This Book Tracker
Belongs

To:

_____

Contact Information:

_____

_____

WARM PUBLISHING
El Paso, Texas
www.warmpublishing.com

Copyright ©2022 Warm Publishing
Interior design by Warm Publishing

ISBN: 978-1-7345961-8-2

All rights reserved. In accordance with the U.S. Copyright Act of 1976, the scanning, uploading and/or electronic sharing of any part of this book without the permission of the publisher constitute unlawful piracy and theft of the author's intellectual property. If you would like to use material from the book (other than for review purposes), prior written permission must be obtained by contacting the publisher at warmpublishing@gmail.com.

Thank you for buying an authorized edition of this book and for complying with copyright laws by not reproducing, scanning, or distributing any part of it in any form without permission. By doing so you are supporting our French authors and allowing Warm Publishing to continue publishing them.

## Table of Contents

How to use this Book Tracker .................................................................... 4
Get´s Started .............................................................................................. 6
Yearly Goals .............................................................................................. 7
Bookshelves ........................................................................................... 8-9
Book Series Tracker ................................................................................ 10
Pages Read this Year .............................................................................. 11
Books Read this Year .............................................................................. 12
January ................................................................................................... 13
February .................................................................................................. 23
March ...................................................................................................... 33
April ........................................................................................................ 43
May ......................................................................................................... 53
June ........................................................................................................ 63
July ......................................................................................................... 73
August .................................................................................................... 83
September .............................................................................................. 93
October ................................................................................................. 103
November ............................................................................................. 113
December ............................................................................................. 123
Final Wrap-up ....................................................................................... 133
Yearly Book Haul ........................................................................... 134-135
Notes .............................................................................................. 136-144

**Please do not use Markers, or any thick pen.**

# HOW TO USE THIS BOOK

This book tracker was created to help avid readers to organize and track their reading.

Warm Publishing will give you some ideas on how you can fill this book tracker, those ideas are just some examples, of course there are thousands of other ways to do it.

You can start this book tracker **anytime of the year.**

**Please note that use of markers, or any thick pen will leave ink marks on the other side of the page.**

You should start by filling the "*Get Started*" page with the books that you have on your TBR (To Be Read) list in order for you to measure your progress at the end of the year. In the section "Other information" you can either add more information about last year, or you can create a legend or a key code that you will follow in this book. Examples:

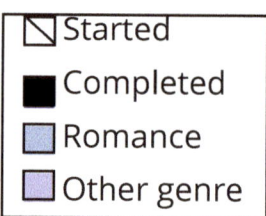

In the "*Yearly Goals*" page, you can add your reading goals, like "read 100 books, read more romance..." you can also add your personal goals, like something you want to accomplish, where you want to travel... there is a lot of content you can add.

The "*Book Series Tracker*" is a great page for the series you want to read and track. We added 8 squares that you can color when you are done. If there are less than 8 books in the series, you can spread the squares according to the number you need.

"*Page Read this Year*" page is the opportunity for you to track the number of pages you have read. You'll have to adjust it according to your own monthly reading page habits. "*Book Read This Year*" pages can be used the same way and are a very good opportunity to use Colorful Washi tape to establish a color code by genres or purpose of reading.

After the yearly pages, you'll discover our monthly pages that you can decorate as you wish. Each month repeats the same pattern.

After each month's cover page, you'll find an *"empty bookshelf"* that you can customize as you like, with the book you want to read, the book you bought, the books that you already have...

Next is the *"To Be Read"* page where you can list the books that you want to read and can be customized with keys, colors, calligraphies...

The *"Reading Challenge"* page is mostly dedicated to challenges that you want to do during the month, but you can easily customize this page. We have added a list of ideas in the page.

The *"New release"* page is for books that you know will be released this specific month and that you are waiting for. You can add the format and where to find it. This page can be filled anytime of the year.

The *"Book Haul"* page is where you can log all the books, e-books and audiobooks that you have purchased this month. You'll also find a page at the end of the year where you can list all the haul that you have made and track them.

The *"Monthly Wrap-Up"* page is where you can log and rate your reads. You'll be able to count pages read, books, e-books, audiobooks, best books, genre read.

You'll find pages where you can *review books*, with all the details you want to remember. If you need more you'll find *Notes* pages at the end that you'll be free to customize. In the reviews pages, we have added rectangles where you can either draw the book cover or add the best quote or else as you wish.

*"Notes"* pages are the opportunity for you to awake your creativity. Indeed you can create any contents.

At the end of the book tracker you'll find your *"Yearly Wrap-Up"* page where you summarize your yearly reading, and get ready for the next year.

**Thank you for choosing Warm Publishing's Book Tracker. We would love to see your creativity. Please share your Book Tracker on social media with @WarmPublishing and #warmpubbooktracker.**

# GET STARTED

**WHEN DID I START THIS JOURNAL:** _____

**HOW MANY BOOKS AM I STARTING THIS YEAR WITH:** _____

**HOW MANY E-BOOKS TBR:** _____

**HOW MANY AUDIOBOOKS:** _____

**HOW MANY BOOKS DID YOU READ LAST YEAR:** _____

**OTHER INFORMATION:**

# YEARLY GOALS

# BOOK SERIES TRACKER

| | BOOK SERIES | BOOK COMPLETED |
|---|---|---|
| | | |

# PAGES READ THIS YEAR

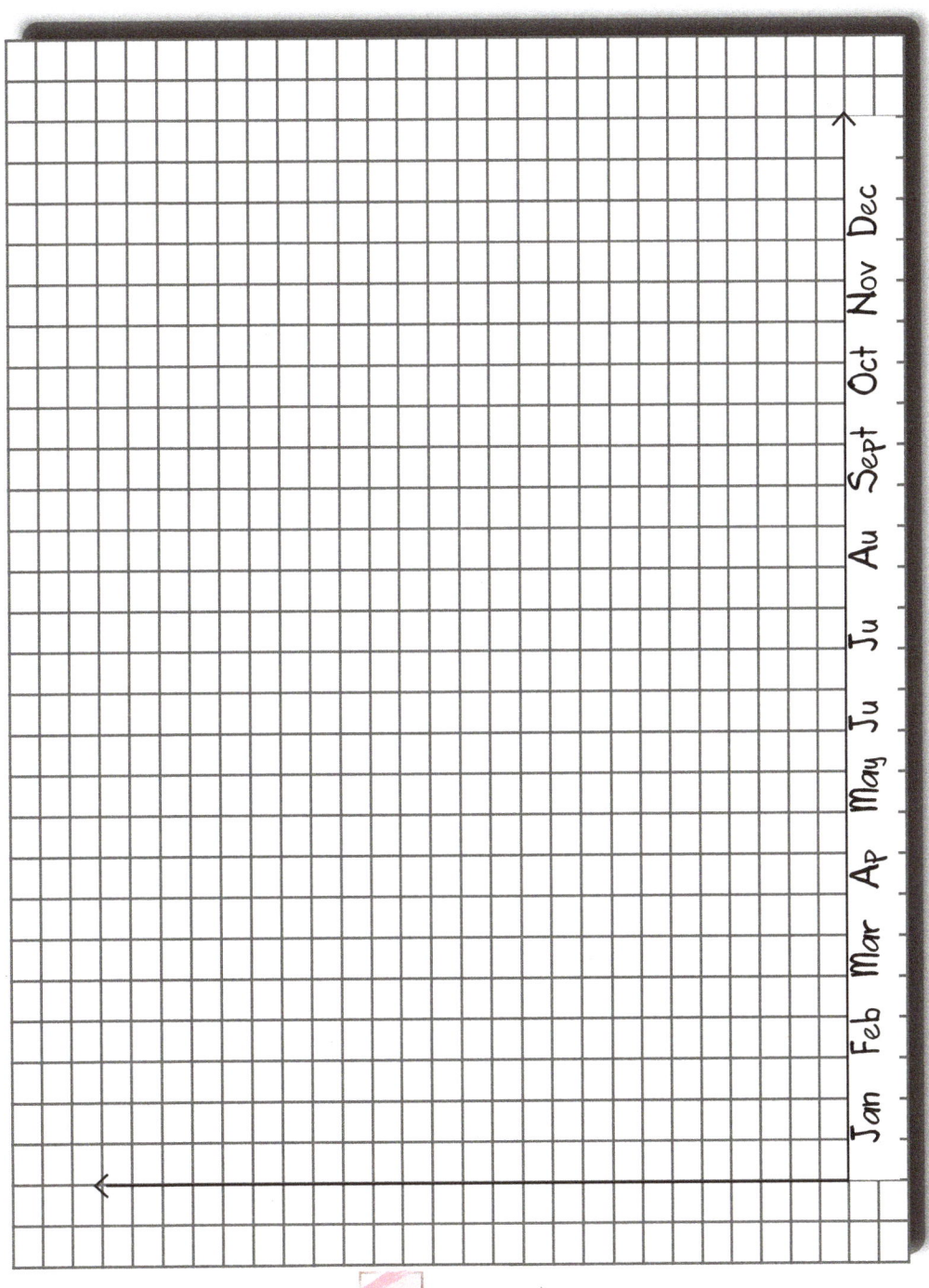

# BOOKS READ THIS YEAR

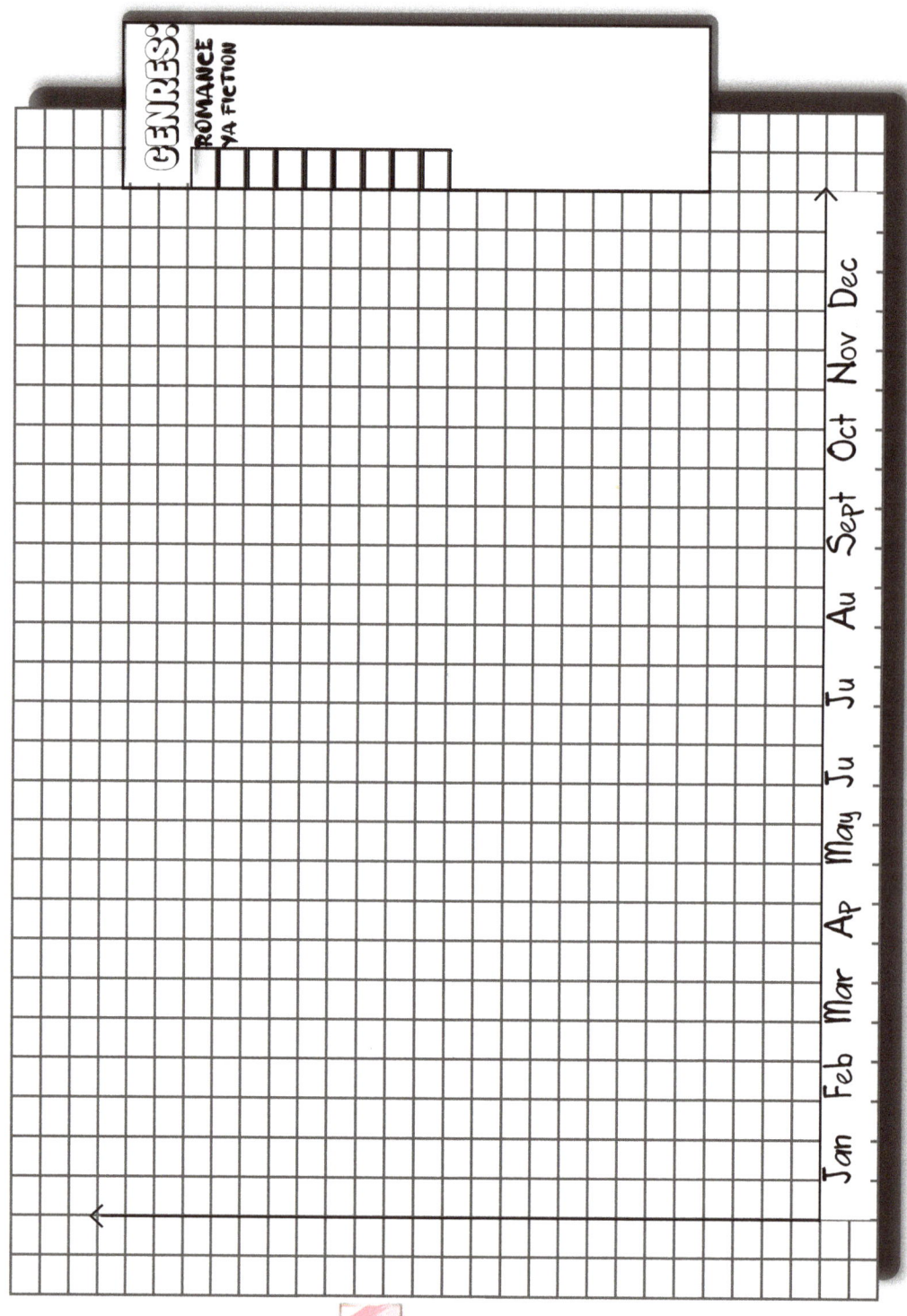

# JANUARY

# Aslo by Warm Publishing
# The Cocky Heir

### by *Ana K. Anderson*

She is about to get married. But not to him.

Quinn MacFayden, an accomplished expat businessman in New York, is set to return to Scotland in extremis to protect the precious family legacy. His 91-year-old grandfather is about to marry a perfect stranger sixty-six years his junior... And that is out of the question! Quinn swears it. Over his dead body will Dawn Fleming ever be part of the family!

But Dawn is not a future bride like the others. She is nowhere near the gold digger he imagined and, above all, she knows just how to stand up to him. And so a game of cat and mouse begins between them. A war with no holds barred and where surrender has never been so tempting...

# BOOKS TO READ

**MONTH:**
**YEAR:**

| AUTHORS | TITLES |
|---------|--------|
|         |        |
|         |        |
|         |        |
|         |        |
|         |        |
|         |        |
|         |        |
|         |        |
|         |        |
|         |        |
|         |        |
|         |        |
|         |        |
|         |        |
|         |        |
|         |        |
|         |        |
|         |        |

# READING CHALLENGES

| ☐ | ☐ |
|---|---|
| ☐ | ☐ |
| ☐ | ☐ |
| ☐ | ☐ |
| ☐ | ☐ |
| ☐ | ☐ |
| ☐ | ☐ |
| ☐ | ☐ |
| ☐ | ☐ |
| ☐ | ☐ |
| ☐ | ☐ |

# NEW RELEASES

| DATE | TITLE |
|------|-------|
|      |       |
|      |       |
|      |       |
|      |       |
|      |       |
|      |       |
|      |       |
|      |       |
|      |       |
|      |       |
|      |       |
|      |       |
|      |       |
|      |       |
|      |       |
|      |       |
|      |       |
|      |       |
|      |       |
|      |       |
|      |       |
|      |       |
|      |       |
|      |       |

# BOOK HAUL

# MONTHLY WRAP-UP

N° OF PAGES READ: _____

N° OF BOOKS READ: _____

N° OF E-BOOKS READ: _____

N° OF AUDIOBOOKS: _____

### BEST BOOKS:
................................................
................................................
................................................
................................................

### GENRES READ:
................................................
................................................
................................................

\* ................................................
☆☆☆☆☆
\* ................................................
☆☆☆☆☆
\* ................................................
☆☆☆☆☆

\* ................................................
☆☆☆☆☆
\* ................................................
☆☆☆☆☆
\* ................................................
☆☆☆☆☆
\* ................................................
☆☆☆☆☆
\* ................................................
☆☆☆☆☆
\* ................................................
☆☆☆☆☆
\* ................................................
☆☆☆☆☆
\* ................................................
☆☆☆☆☆
\* ................................................
☆☆☆☆☆
\* ................................................
☆☆☆☆☆

# BOOK REVIEWS

TITLE:  AUTHOR:

GENRE:  N° OF PAGES:

RATING: ☆☆☆☆☆ FORMAT:

REVIEW:

---

TITLE:  AUTHOR:

GENRE:  N° OF PAGES:

RATING: ☆☆☆☆☆ FORMAT:

REVIEW:

# BOOK REVIEWS

**TITLE:**        **AUTHOR:**

**GENRE:**       **N° OF PAGES:**

**RATING:** ☆☆☆☆☆ **FORMAT:**

**REVIEW:**

---

**TITLE:**        **AUTHOR:**

**GENRE:**       **N° OF PAGES:**

**RATING:** ☆☆☆☆☆ **FORMAT:**

**REVIEW:**

# NOTES

# FEBRUARY

Aslo by Warm Publishing

# Falling for the Voice

by *Mag Maury*

The sexiest of surprises... and the most unbearable!

My plan was simple: Find a job quickly in order to make rent. And I found one. A waitressing job at the hottest pub in town!

Everything was going smoothly until he arrived: Matt. Sexy. Arrogant. Six feet three of muscles that drive women into a hysterical frenzy at every single one of his concerts.

This guy is really comfortable on stage and oh, so enticing. We girls can try to put him out of our minds but we end up wanting him anyway. And he knows it.

Except me, Charlotte. I say no!

Well... Maybe! After all, I have never really been good at resisting temptation...

# BOOKS TO READ

**MONTH:**
**YEAR:**

| AUTHORS | TITLES |
|---------|--------|
|         |        |
|         |        |
|         |        |
|         |        |
|         |        |
|         |        |
|         |        |
|         |        |
|         |        |
|         |        |
|         |        |
|         |        |
|         |        |
|         |        |
|         |        |
|         |        |
|         |        |
|         |        |

# READING CHALLENGES

- [ ] _____
- [ ] _____
- [ ] _____
- [ ] _____
- [ ] _____
- [ ] _____
- [ ] _____
- [ ] _____
- [ ] _____
- [ ] _____
- [ ] _____

- [ ] _____
- [ ] _____
- [ ] _____
- [ ] _____
- [ ] _____
- [ ] _____
- [ ] _____
- [ ] _____
- [ ] _____
- [ ] _____
- [ ] _____

# NEW RELEASES

| DATE | TITLE |
|------|-------|
|      |       |
|      |       |
|      |       |
|      |       |
|      |       |
|      |       |
|      |       |
|      |       |
|      |       |
|      |       |
|      |       |
|      |       |
|      |       |
|      |       |
|      |       |
|      |       |
|      |       |
|      |       |
|      |       |
|      |       |
|      |       |
|      |       |
|      |       |
|      |       |
|      |       |

# BOOK HAUL

# MONTHLY WRAP-UP

N° OF PAGES READ: _____

N° OF BOOKS READ: _____

N° OF E-BOOKS READ: _____

N° OF AUDIOBOOKS: _____

### BEST BOOKS:
..................................................
..................................................
..................................................
..................................................

### GENRES READ:
..................................................
..................................................
..................................................
..................................................

* ..................................................
  ☆☆☆☆☆
* ..................................................
  ☆☆☆☆☆
* ..................................................
  ☆☆☆☆☆

* ..................................................
  ☆☆☆☆☆
* ..................................................
  ☆☆☆☆☆
* ..................................................
  ☆☆☆☆☆
* ..................................................
  ☆☆☆☆☆
* ..................................................
  ☆☆☆☆☆
* ..................................................
  ☆☆☆☆☆
* ..................................................
  ☆☆☆☆☆
* ..................................................
  ☆☆☆☆☆
* ..................................................
  ☆☆☆☆☆
* ..................................................
  ☆☆☆☆☆
* ..................................................
  ☆☆☆☆☆

# BOOK REVIEWS

TITLE:  AUTHOR:

GENRE:  N° OF PAGES:

RATING: ☆☆☆☆☆  FORMAT:

REVIEW:

---

TITLE:  AUTHOR:

GENRE:  N° OF PAGES:

RATING: ☆☆☆☆☆  FORMAT:

REVIEW:

# BOOK REVIEWS

**TITLE:**         **AUTHOR:**

**GENRE:**        **N° OF PAGES:**

**RATING:** ☆☆☆☆☆ **FORMAT:**

**REVIEW:**

---

**TITLE:**         **AUTHOR:**

**GENRE:**        **N° OF PAGES:**

**RATING:** ☆☆☆☆☆ **FORMAT:**

**REVIEW:**

# NOTES

# MARCH

Aslo by Warm Publishing
# My Stepbrother: A Sexual Revelation

by *Sophie S. Pierucci*

Cassie is a highly intelligent young woman... Too much so for her own good! And she is as daunting as she is intriguing. Carl, the son of his father's second wife, would hardly say otherwise!

Carl is the exact opposite of his steady father. He is a player and a slayer. Afraid of nothing and no one. Except for Cassie when she asks him to introduce her to the pleasures of the flesh.

And when the situation gets out of control, it is too late to turn back, and the two lovers find themselves ensnared in forbidden passion. Forbidden by everyone: society, their parents, their friends.

But how to resist the desire that consumes them?

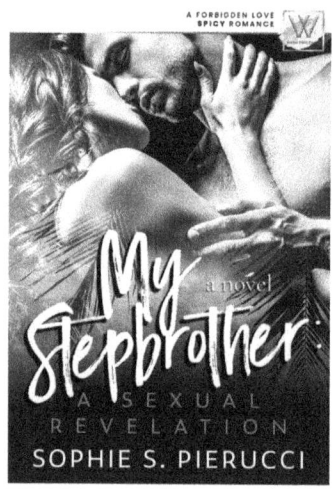

# BOOKS TO READ

**MONTH:**
**YEAR:**

| AUTHORS | TITLES |
|---------|--------|
|         |        |
|         |        |
|         |        |
|         |        |
|         |        |
|         |        |
|         |        |
|         |        |
|         |        |
|         |        |
|         |        |
|         |        |
|         |        |
|         |        |
|         |        |
|         |        |
|         |        |
|         |        |
|         |        |

# READING CHALLENGES

☐ | ☐
--- | ---
☐ | ☐
☐ | ☐
☐ | ☐
☐ | ☐
☐ | ☐
☐ | ☐
☐ | ☐
☐ | ☐
☐ | ☐
☐ | ☐

# NEW RELEASES

| DATE | TITLE |
|------|-------|
|      |       |
|      |       |
|      |       |
|      |       |
|      |       |
|      |       |
|      |       |
|      |       |
|      |       |
|      |       |
|      |       |
|      |       |
|      |       |
|      |       |
|      |       |
|      |       |
|      |       |
|      |       |
|      |       |
|      |       |
|      |       |
|      |       |

# BOOK HAUL

# MONTHLY WRAP-UP

N° OF PAGES READ: _____

N° OF BOOKS READ: _____

N° OF E-BOOKS READ: _____

N° OF AUDIOBOOKS: _____

## BEST BOOKS:
..................................................
..................................................
..................................................
..................................................

## GENRES READ:
..................................................
..................................................
..................................................
..................................................

\* ..................................................
☆☆☆☆☆
\* ..................................................
☆☆☆☆☆
\* ..................................................
☆☆☆☆☆

\* ..................................................
☆☆☆☆☆
\* ..................................................
☆☆☆☆☆
\* ..................................................
☆☆☆☆☆
\* ..................................................
☆☆☆☆☆
\* ..................................................
☆☆☆☆☆
\* ..................................................
☆☆☆☆☆
\* ..................................................
☆☆☆☆☆
\* ..................................................
☆☆☆☆☆
\* ..................................................
☆☆☆☆☆
\* ..................................................
☆☆☆☆☆
\* ..................................................
☆☆☆☆☆

# BOOK REVIEWS

**TITLE:**  **AUTHOR:**

**GENRE:**  **N° OF PAGES:**

**RATING:** ☆☆☆☆☆  **FORMAT:**

**REVIEW:**

---

**TITLE:**  **AUTHOR:**

**GENRE:**  **N° OF PAGES:**

**RATING:** ☆☆☆☆☆  **FORMAT:**

**REVIEW:**

# BOOK REVIEWS

**TITLE:**  **AUTHOR:**

**GENRE:**  **N° OF PAGES:**

**RATING:** ☆☆☆☆☆ **FORMAT:**

**REVIEW:**

---

**TITLE:**  **AUTHOR:**

**GENRE:**  **N° OF PAGES:**

**RATING:** ☆☆☆☆☆ **FORMAT:**

**REVIEW:**

# NOTES

# APRIL

Aslo by Warm Publishing
# My Hipster Next Door

### by *Mag Maury*

In Liverpool, the barbershop Hipster Maniac is an institution. Run by three bearded, tattooed friends, it is the place to listen to great rock, get a trim, and have a drink.

But for Line, it also spelled trouble. For starters, when she first got to the neighborhood, she rear-ended Jordan's car, who turned out to be one of the three barbers. Then she discovered that they were neighbors in business and residence! So no way can she escape this muscle-flaunting, smoldering man who is covered in tattoos and... completely insufferable!

He draws her near only to push her away. He toys with her shamelessly. But worst of all he hates Christmas whereas that is Line's very favorite time of year!

Beneath a backdrop of festive fairy lights, intoxicatingly passionate kisses, and blistering banter... It's on!

# BOOKS TO READ

**MONTH:**
**YEAR:**

| AUTHORS | TITLES |
|---------|--------|
|         |        |
|         |        |
|         |        |
|         |        |
|         |        |
|         |        |
|         |        |
|         |        |
|         |        |
|         |        |
|         |        |
|         |        |
|         |        |
|         |        |
|         |        |
|         |        |
|         |        |

# READING CHALLENGES

# NEW RELEASES

| DATE | TITLE |
|------|-------|
|      |       |
|      |       |
|      |       |
|      |       |
|      |       |
|      |       |
|      |       |
|      |       |
|      |       |
|      |       |
|      |       |
|      |       |
|      |       |
|      |       |
|      |       |
|      |       |
|      |       |
|      |       |
|      |       |
|      |       |
|      |       |
|      |       |

# BOOK HAUL

# MONTHLY WRAP-UP

N° OF PAGES READ: _____

N° OF BOOKS READ: _____

N° OF E-BOOKS READ: _____

N° OF AUDIOBOOKS: _____

## BEST BOOKS:
...........................................
...........................................
...........................................
...........................................

## GENRES READ:
...........................................
...........................................
...........................................

* ...........................................
  ☆☆☆☆☆
* ...........................................
  ☆☆☆☆☆
* ...........................................
  ☆☆☆☆☆

* ...........................................
  ☆☆☆☆☆
* ...........................................
  ☆☆☆☆☆
* ...........................................
  ☆☆☆☆☆
* ...........................................
  ☆☆☆☆☆
* ...........................................
  ☆☆☆☆☆
* ...........................................
  ☆☆☆☆☆
* ...........................................
  ☆☆☆☆☆
* ...........................................
  ☆☆☆☆☆
* ...........................................
  ☆☆☆☆☆
* ...........................................
  ☆☆☆☆☆
* ...........................................
  ☆☆☆☆☆

# BOOK REVIEWS

TITLE:     AUTHOR:

GENRE:     N° OF PAGES:

RATING: ☆☆☆☆☆   FORMAT:

REVIEW:

---

TITLE:     AUTHOR:

GENRE:     N° OF PAGES:

RATING: ☆☆☆☆☆   FORMAT:

REVIEW:

# BOOK REVIEWS

TITLE:  AUTHOR:

GENRE:  N° OF PAGES:

RATING: ☆☆☆☆☆ FORMAT:

REVIEW:

---

TITLE:  AUTHOR:

GENRE:  N° OF PAGES:

RATING: ☆☆☆☆☆ FORMAT:

REVIEW:

# NOTES

# MAY

Aslo by Warm Publishing
# Roommate with my Boss
### by *Erin Graham*

Boss, roommate, fake fiancé... real lover?
Étienne is cold, charismatic, and he never shies away from a challenge.
He masters everything down to the smallest detail... until a little accountant with an unlikely look and flowers in her hair inserts herself into his daily life.
She is whimsical, full of life, laughs at the rules and gets around them, talks all the time except about her past... and she drives him crazy. Yet, it's impossible to fire her.
She needs a job and a roof over her head; he needs a fake fiancée...
Is it a deal?

# BOOKS TO READ

**MONTH:**
**YEAR:**

| AUTHORS | TITLES |
|---------|--------|
|         |        |
|         |        |
|         |        |
|         |        |
|         |        |
|         |        |
|         |        |
|         |        |
|         |        |
|         |        |
|         |        |
|         |        |
|         |        |
|         |        |
|         |        |
|         |        |
|         |        |
|         |        |

# READING CHALLENGES

# NEW RELEASES

| DATE | TITLE |
|------|-------|
|      |       |
|      |       |
|      |       |
|      |       |
|      |       |
|      |       |
|      |       |
|      |       |
|      |       |
|      |       |
|      |       |
|      |       |
|      |       |
|      |       |
|      |       |
|      |       |
|      |       |
|      |       |
|      |       |
|      |       |
|      |       |
|      |       |
|      |       |
|      |       |

# BOOK HAUL

# MONTHLY WRAP-UP

N° OF PAGES READ: _____

N° OF BOOKS READ: _____

N° OF E-BOOKS READ: _____

N° OF AUDIOBOOKS: _____

## BEST BOOKS:
................................
................................
................................
................................

## GENRES READ:
................................
................................
................................
................................

* ................................ ☆☆☆☆☆
* ................................ ☆☆☆☆☆
* ................................ ☆☆☆☆☆
* ................................ ☆☆☆☆☆
* ................................ ☆☆☆☆☆
* ................................ ☆☆☆☆☆
* ................................ ☆☆☆☆☆
* ................................ ☆☆☆☆☆
* ................................ ☆☆☆☆☆
* ................................ ☆☆☆☆☆
* ................................ ☆☆☆☆☆
* ................................ ☆☆☆☆☆
* ................................ ☆☆☆☆☆
* ................................ ☆☆☆☆☆
* ................................ ☆☆☆☆☆
* ................................ ☆☆☆☆☆

# BOOK REVIEWS

**TITLE:**  **AUTHOR:**

**GENRE:**  **N° OF PAGES:**

**RATING:** ☆☆☆☆☆ **FORMAT:**

**REVIEW:**

---

**TITLE:**  **AUTHOR:**

**GENRE:**  **N° OF PAGES:**

**RATING:** ☆☆☆☆☆ **FORMAT:**

**REVIEW:**

# BOOK REVIEWS

TITLE:  AUTHOR:

GENRE:  N° OF PAGES:

RATING: ☆☆☆☆☆ FORMAT:

REVIEW:

---

TITLE:  AUTHOR:

GENRE:  N° OF PAGES:

RATING: ☆☆☆☆☆ FORMAT:

REVIEW:

# NOTES

# JUNE

Aslo by Warm Publishing
# Damn Roommate
by *Lou Garance*

**Falling for your brother's best friend? Not a good idea!**
**Moving in with him? Even worse!**

When she moves in with her brother's roommate and his group of friends, Scarlett feels like she's really in for it.

She couldn't get Nolan Jones out of her head while living thousands of miles away from him, so how could she possibly forget him now that she's back in Boston? Especially now that she occupies the room right next to his?

Yet her lifelong crush gives her no reason to hope. Nolan teases her like she's his little sister! Scarlett knows she has to accept that he will never see her otherwise.

But between the evenings spent challenging each other, the unsettling closeness on the couch and the new spark she sees in Nolan's eyes, never might be coming sooner rather than later.

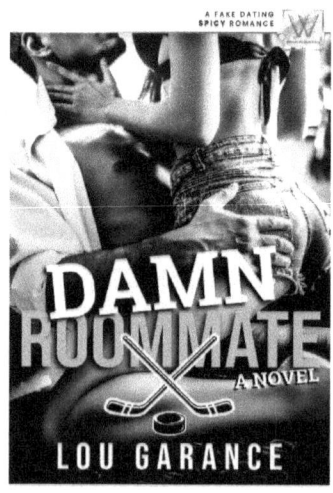

# BOOKS TO READ

**MONTH:**
**YEAR:**

| AUTHORS | TITLES |
|---------|--------|
|         |        |
|         |        |
|         |        |
|         |        |
|         |        |
|         |        |
|         |        |
|         |        |
|         |        |
|         |        |
|         |        |
|         |        |
|         |        |
|         |        |
|         |        |
|         |        |
|         |        |

# READING CHALLENGES

# NEW RELEASES

| DATE | TITLE |
|------|-------|
|      |       |
|      |       |
|      |       |
|      |       |
|      |       |
|      |       |
|      |       |
|      |       |
|      |       |
|      |       |
|      |       |
|      |       |
|      |       |
|      |       |
|      |       |
|      |       |
|      |       |
|      |       |
|      |       |
|      |       |
|      |       |
|      |       |

# BOOK HAUL

# MONTHLY WRAP-UP

N° OF PAGES READ: _____

N° OF BOOKS READ: _____

N° OF E-BOOKS READ: _____

N° OF AUDIOBOOKS: _____

### BEST BOOKS:
....................................................
....................................................
....................................................
....................................................

### GENRES READ:
....................................................
....................................................
....................................................

* ..................................................
  ☆☆☆☆☆
* ..................................................
  ☆☆☆☆☆
* ..................................................
  ☆☆☆☆☆

* ..................................................
  ☆☆☆☆☆
* ..................................................
  ☆☆☆☆☆
* ..................................................
  ☆☆☆☆☆
* ..................................................
  ☆☆☆☆☆
* ..................................................
  ☆☆☆☆☆
* ..................................................
  ☆☆☆☆☆
* ..................................................
  ☆☆☆☆☆
* ..................................................
  ☆☆☆☆☆
* ..................................................
  ☆☆☆☆☆
* ..................................................
  ☆☆☆☆☆
* ..................................................
  ☆☆☆☆☆
* ..................................................
  ☆☆☆☆☆

# BOOK REVIEWS

**TITLE:**         **AUTHOR:**

**GENRE:**        **N° OF PAGES:**

**RATING:** ☆☆☆☆☆ **FORMAT:**

**REVIEW:**

---

**TITLE:**         **AUTHOR:**

**GENRE:**        **N° OF PAGES:**

**RATING:** ☆☆☆☆☆ **FORMAT:**

**REVIEW:**

# BOOK REVIEWS

**TITLE:**          **AUTHOR:**

**GENRE:**         **N° OF PAGES:**

**RATING:** ☆☆☆☆☆ **FORMAT:**

**REVIEW:**

---

**TITLE:**          **AUTHOR:**

**GENRE:**         **N° OF PAGES:**

**RATING:** ☆☆☆☆☆ **FORMAT:**

**REVIEW:**

# NOTES

# JULY

Aslo by Warm Publishing
# Your Power Over Me
by *Missy Heart*

**A family home heavy with secrets, a dangerously charismatic owner.**

Will her arrival at Iron House be the end of her?

Ever since she was a teenager, Lovisa has known it: at Iron House, anything can happen, especially the worst.

However, when she is forced to return to the family home for her stepfather's funeral, her heart races: she is going to see him again, this "brother" who she never wanted and who yet turned her whole world upside down.

Now at the head of a drug cartel, authoritarian and brutal, Niklas is nothing like the teenager she knew nine years ago. At his side, Lovisa finds herself immersed in a harsh, ruthless—but fascinating—world.

Irremediably attracted to this man who wants her as much harm as good, will Lovisa manage to fight her unmentionable desires? Or will she give in to Niklas' magnetic darkness?

# BOOKS TO READ

**MONTH:**
**YEAR:**

| AUTHORS | TITLES |
|---------|--------|
|         |        |
|         |        |
|         |        |
|         |        |
|         |        |
|         |        |
|         |        |
|         |        |
|         |        |
|         |        |
|         |        |
|         |        |
|         |        |
|         |        |
|         |        |
|         |        |
|         |        |
|         |        |

# READING CHALLENGES

# NEW RELEASES

| DATE | TITLE |
|------|-------|
|      |       |
|      |       |
|      |       |
|      |       |
|      |       |
|      |       |
|      |       |
|      |       |
|      |       |
|      |       |
|      |       |
|      |       |
|      |       |
|      |       |
|      |       |
|      |       |
|      |       |
|      |       |
|      |       |
|      |       |
|      |       |
|      |       |
|      |       |

# BOOK HAUL

# MONTHLY WRAP-UP

N° OF PAGES READ: _____

N° OF BOOKS READ: _____

N° OF E-BOOKS READ: _____

N° OF AUDIOBOOKS: _____

## BEST BOOKS:
..............................
..............................
..............................
..............................

## GENRES READ:
..............................
..............................
..............................
..............................

* ..............................
  ☆☆☆☆☆
* ..............................
  ☆☆☆☆☆
* ..............................
  ☆☆☆☆☆

* ..............................
  ☆☆☆☆☆
* ..............................
  ☆☆☆☆☆
* ..............................
  ☆☆☆☆☆
* ..............................
  ☆☆☆☆☆
* ..............................
  ☆☆☆☆☆
* ..............................
  ☆☆☆☆☆
* ..............................
  ☆☆☆☆☆
* ..............................
  ☆☆☆☆☆
* ..............................
  ☆☆☆☆☆
* ..............................
  ☆☆☆☆☆
* ..............................
  ☆☆☆☆☆
* ..............................
  ☆☆☆☆☆

# BOOK REVIEWS

**TITLE:** **AUTHOR:**

**GENRE:** **N° OF PAGES:**

**RATING:** ☆☆☆☆☆ **FORMAT:**

**REVIEW:**

---

**TITLE:** **AUTHOR:**

**GENRE:** **N° OF PAGES:**

**RATING:** ☆☆☆☆☆ **FORMAT:**

**REVIEW:**

# BOOK REVIEWS

**TITLE:** **AUTHOR:**

**GENRE:** **N° OF PAGES:**

**RATING:** ☆☆☆☆☆ **FORMAT:**

**REVIEW:**

---

**TITLE:** **AUTHOR:**

**GENRE:** **N° OF PAGES:**

**RATING:** ☆☆☆☆☆ **FORMAT:**

**REVIEW:**

# NOTES

# AUGUST

# Aslo by Warm Publishing
# Touchdown
### by *Sonia Birdy*

**She's a runner, but the campus star quaterback runs faster than she does!**

Rocky has had a chaotic life from which she concluded three fundamental things: life is a succession of problems to be solved, men are assholes to be avoided and promises are only binding on fools who want to believe in them. So, unlike the other girls on campus, boys are not a priority for her. Worse, she sees them as an obstacle to her success!

But during a student party, she meets Jude. Freshly transferred from Harvard to play on Brown's soccer team, Jude is the new star on campus. Handsome and inaccessible, he is the type not to get attached: the perfect candidate for a one-night stand.

But the chemistry is too strong. And though Rocky is determined to run away from him, he is determined to conquer her heart.

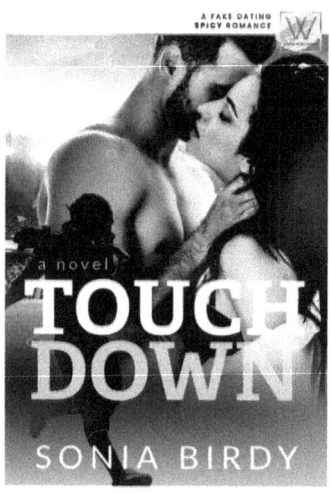

# BOOKS TO READ

**MONTH:**
**YEAR:**

| AUTHORS | TITLES |
|---------|--------|
|         |        |
|         |        |
|         |        |
|         |        |
|         |        |
|         |        |
|         |        |
|         |        |
|         |        |
|         |        |
|         |        |
|         |        |
|         |        |
|         |        |
|         |        |
|         |        |
|         |        |
|         |        |

# READING CHALLENGES

# NEW RELEASES

| DATE | TITLE |
|------|-------|
|      |       |
|      |       |
|      |       |
|      |       |
|      |       |
|      |       |
|      |       |
|      |       |
|      |       |
|      |       |
|      |       |
|      |       |
|      |       |
|      |       |
|      |       |
|      |       |
|      |       |
|      |       |
|      |       |
|      |       |
|      |       |
|      |       |
|      |       |
|      |       |

# BOOK HAUL

# MONTHLY WRAP-UP

N° OF PAGES READ: _____

N° OF BOOKS READ: _____

N° OF E-BOOKS READ: _____

N° OF AUDIOBOOKS: _____

## BEST BOOKS:
..............................................
..............................................
..............................................
..............................................

## GENRES READ:
..............................................
..............................................
..............................................

\* ..............................................
☆☆☆☆☆
\* ..............................................
☆☆☆☆☆
\* ..............................................
☆☆☆☆☆

\* ..............................................
☆☆☆☆☆
\* ..............................................
☆☆☆☆☆
\* ..............................................
☆☆☆☆☆
\* ..............................................
☆☆☆☆☆
\* ..............................................
☆☆☆☆☆
\* ..............................................
☆☆☆☆☆
\* ..............................................
☆☆☆☆☆
\* ..............................................
☆☆☆☆☆
\* ..............................................
☆☆☆☆☆
\* ..............................................
☆☆☆☆☆
\* ..............................................
☆☆☆☆☆
\* ..............................................
☆☆☆☆☆

# BOOK REVIEWS

**TITLE:**  **AUTHOR:**

**GENRE:**  **N° OF PAGES:**

**RATING:** ☆☆☆☆☆ **FORMAT:**

**REVIEW:**

---

**TITLE:**  **AUTHOR:**

**GENRE:**  **N° OF PAGES:**

**RATING:** ☆☆☆☆☆ **FORMAT:**

**REVIEW:**

# BOOK REVIEWS

TITLE:   AUTHOR:

GENRE:   N° OF PAGES:

RATING: ☆☆☆☆☆ FORMAT:

REVIEW:

---

TITLE:   AUTHOR:

GENRE:   N° OF PAGES:

RATING: ☆☆☆☆☆ FORMAT:

REVIEW:

# NOTES

# SEPTEMBER

Aslo by Warm Publishing
# Private Garden
by *Oly TL*

**The most disturbing and transgressive of contracts...**

Tiger Sexton seems to have it all. Charisma. Respect. Relentless business acumen. More fortune than he could spend in a life and a sublime wife, Sophia.

When Oceane is invited by Mrs. Sexton for a job interview in one of the restaurants that her husband gave her, the young French tourist knows nothing about this couple. Their name means
nothing to her, people are not her thing. She just wants a job, a place to live and to move on with her life... Sophia's proposal comes at the right time: the Sextons are looking for an *au pair*.

But by opening their doors to her, many other locks are likely to open. Is Oceane ready for this? And what about Sophia, and especially the Tiger lurking in this Secret Garden?

# BOOKS TO READ

MONTH:
YEAR:

| AUTHORS | TITLES |
|---|---|
| | |
| | |
| | |
| | |
| | |
| | |
| | |
| | |
| | |
| | |
| | |
| | |
| | |
| | |
| | |
| | |
| | |
| | |
| | |

# READING CHALLENGES

- [ ] 
- [ ] 
- [ ] 
- [ ] 
- [ ] 
- [ ] 
- [ ] 
- [ ] 
- [ ] 
- [ ] 
- [ ] 
- [ ] 
- [ ] 
- [ ] 
- [ ] 
- [ ] 
- [ ] 
- [ ] 
- [ ] 
- [ ] 
- [ ] 
- [ ] 

# NEW RELEASES

| DATE | TITLE |
|------|-------|
|      |       |
|      |       |
|      |       |
|      |       |
|      |       |
|      |       |
|      |       |
|      |       |
|      |       |
|      |       |
|      |       |
|      |       |
|      |       |
|      |       |
|      |       |
|      |       |
|      |       |
|      |       |
|      |       |
|      |       |
|      |       |
|      |       |
|      |       |

# BOOK HAUL

# MONTHLY WRAP-UP

N° OF PAGES READ: _____

N° OF BOOKS READ: _____

N° OF E-BOOKS READ: _____

N° OF AUDIOBOOKS: _____

### BEST BOOKS:
........................................................
........................................................
........................................................
........................................................

### GENRES READ:
........................................................
........................................................
........................................................
........................................................

\* ........................................................
☆☆☆☆☆
\* ........................................................
☆☆☆☆☆
\* ........................................................
☆☆☆☆☆

\* ........................................................
☆☆☆☆☆
\* ........................................................
☆☆☆☆☆
\* ........................................................
☆☆☆☆☆
\* ........................................................
☆☆☆☆☆
\* ........................................................
☆☆☆☆☆
\* ........................................................
☆☆☆☆☆
\* ........................................................
☆☆☆☆☆
\* ........................................................
☆☆☆☆☆
\* ........................................................
☆☆☆☆☆
\* ........................................................
☆☆☆☆☆
\* ........................................................
☆☆☆☆☆
\* ........................................................
☆☆☆☆☆
\* ........................................................
☆☆☆☆☆

# BOOK REVIEWS

**TITLE:** **AUTHOR:**

**GENRE:** **N° OF PAGES:**

**RATING:** ☆☆☆☆☆ **FORMAT:**

**REVIEW:**

---

**TITLE:** **AUTHOR:**

**GENRE:** **N° OF PAGES:**

**RATING:** ☆☆☆☆☆ **FORMAT:**

**REVIEW:**

# BOOK REVIEWS

**TITLE:**       **AUTHOR:**

**GENRE:**      **N° OF PAGES:**

**RATING:** ☆☆☆☆☆ **FORMAT:**

**REVIEW:**

---

**TITLE:**       **AUTHOR:**

**GENRE:**      **N° OF PAGES:**

**RATING:** ☆☆☆☆☆ **FORMAT:**

**REVIEW:**

# NOTES

# OCTOBER

Aslo by Warm Publishing
# The Courtesan Queen
by *Anna Triss*

**She's a runner, but the campus star quaterback runs faster than she does!**

Rocky has had a chaotic life from which she concluded three fundamental things: life is a succession of problems to be solved, men are assholes to be avoided and promises are only binding on fools who want to believe in them. So, unlike the other girls on campus, boys are not a priority for her. Worse, she sees them as an obstacle to her success!

But during a student party, she meets Jude. Freshly transferred from Harvard to play on Brown's soccer team, Jude is the new star on campus. Handsome and inaccessible, he is the type not to get attached: the perfect candidate for a one-night stand.

But the chemistry is too strong. And though Rocky is determined to run away from him, he is determined to conquer her heart.

# BOOKS TO READ

**MONTH:**
**YEAR:**

| AUTHORS | TITLES |
|---------|--------|
|         |        |
|         |        |
|         |        |
|         |        |
|         |        |
|         |        |
|         |        |
|         |        |
|         |        |
|         |        |
|         |        |
|         |        |
|         |        |
|         |        |
|         |        |
|         |        |
|         |        |
|         |        |

# READING CHALLENGES

| ☐ | ☐ |
|---|---|
| ☐ | ☐ |
| ☐ | ☐ |
| ☐ | ☐ |
| ☐ | ☐ |
| ☐ | ☐ |
| ☐ | ☐ |
| ☐ | ☐ |
| ☐ | ☐ |
| ☐ | ☐ |
| ☐ | ☐ |

# NEW RELEASES

| DATE | TITLE |
|------|-------|
|      |       |
|      |       |
|      |       |
|      |       |
|      |       |
|      |       |
|      |       |
|      |       |
|      |       |
|      |       |
|      |       |
|      |       |
|      |       |
|      |       |
|      |       |
|      |       |
|      |       |
|      |       |
|      |       |
|      |       |
|      |       |
|      |       |
|      |       |
|      |       |

# BOOK HAUL

# MONTHLY WRAP-UP

N° OF PAGES READ: _____

N° OF BOOKS READ: _____

N° OF E-BOOKS READ: _____

N° OF AUDIOBOOKS: _____

### BEST BOOKS:
..........................................................
..........................................................
..........................................................
..........................................................

### GENRES READ:
..........................................................
..........................................................
..........................................................

* ........................................................
  ☆☆☆☆☆
* ........................................................
  ☆☆☆☆☆
* ........................................................
  ☆☆☆☆☆

* ........................................................
  ☆☆☆☆☆
* ........................................................
  ☆☆☆☆☆
* ........................................................
  ☆☆☆☆☆
* ........................................................
  ☆☆☆☆☆
* ........................................................
  ☆☆☆☆☆
* ........................................................
  ☆☆☆☆☆
* ........................................................
  ☆☆☆☆☆
* ........................................................
  ☆☆☆☆☆
* ........................................................
  ☆☆☆☆☆
* ........................................................
  ☆☆☆☆☆
* ........................................................
  ☆☆☆☆☆
* ........................................................
  ☆☆☆☆☆

# BOOK REVIEWS

**TITLE:** **AUTHOR:**

**GENRE:** **N° OF PAGES:**

**RATING:** ☆☆☆☆☆ **FORMAT:**

**REVIEW:**

---

**TITLE:** **AUTHOR:**

**GENRE:** **N° OF PAGES:**

**RATING:** ☆☆☆☆☆ **FORMAT:**

**REVIEW:**

# BOOK REVIEWS

**TITLE:** **AUTHOR:**

**GENRE:** **N° OF PAGES:**

**RATING:** ☆☆☆☆☆ **FORMAT:**

**REVIEW:**

---

**TITLE:** **AUTHOR:**

**GENRE:** **N° OF PAGES:**

**RATING:** ☆☆☆☆☆ **FORMAT:**

**REVIEW:**

# NOTES

# NOVEMBER

Aslo by Warm Publishing
# Forbidden Temptation
### by *Samantha Morgan*

**One encounter, three loves at first sight.**

When Craig sees Camille for the first time, he does not realize that he has a crush on her, and she on him. His best friend Julien, on the other hand, does everything to seduce the beauty.

When he comes back to town ten years later, Craig moves in with the couple, altough he never really managed to forget Camille.

In any event, it's too late to make her his.

But a vacation with friends reveals long-buried secrets. Camille is not happy in her relationship, and the presence of Craig, whose gaze destabilizes her, doesn't help the situation...

# BOOKS TO READ

**MONTH:**
**YEAR:**

| AUTHORS | TITLES |
|---------|--------|
|         |        |
|         |        |
|         |        |
|         |        |
|         |        |
|         |        |
|         |        |
|         |        |
|         |        |
|         |        |
|         |        |
|         |        |
|         |        |
|         |        |
|         |        |
|         |        |
|         |        |
|         |        |

# READING CHALLENGES

| ☐ | ☐ |
|---|---|
| ☐ | ☐ |
| ☐ | ☐ |
| ☐ | ☐ |
| ☐ | ☐ |
| ☐ | ☐ |
| ☐ | ☐ |
| ☐ | ☐ |
| ☐ | ☐ |
| ☐ | ☐ |
| ☐ | ☐ |

# NEW RELEASES

| DATE | TITLE |
|---|---|
|  |  |
|  |  |
|  |  |
|  |  |
|  |  |
|  |  |
|  |  |
|  |  |
|  |  |
|  |  |
|  |  |
|  |  |
|  |  |
|  |  |
|  |  |
|  |  |
|  |  |
|  |  |
|  |  |
|  |  |
|  |  |
|  |  |
|  |  |
|  |  |

# BOOK HAUL

# MONTHLY WRAP-UP

N° OF PAGES READ: _____

N° OF BOOKS READ: _____

N° OF E-BOOKS READ: _____

N° OF AUDIOBOOKS: _____

### BEST BOOKS:

..............................................
..............................................
..............................................
..............................................

### GENRES READ:

..............................................
..............................................
..............................................

\* ..............................................
☆☆☆☆☆
\* ..............................................
☆☆☆☆☆
\* ..............................................
☆☆☆☆☆

\* ..............................................
☆☆☆☆☆
\* ..............................................
☆☆☆☆☆
\* ..............................................
☆☆☆☆☆
\* ..............................................
☆☆☆☆☆
\* ..............................................
☆☆☆☆☆
\* ..............................................
☆☆☆☆☆
\* ..............................................
☆☆☆☆☆
\* ..............................................
☆☆☆☆☆
\* ..............................................
☆☆☆☆☆
\* ..............................................
☆☆☆☆☆
\* ..............................................
☆☆☆☆☆
\* ..............................................
☆☆☆☆☆

# BOOK REVIEWS

**TITLE:**            **AUTHOR:**

**GENRE:**            **N° OF PAGES:**

**RATING:** ☆☆☆☆☆ **FORMAT:**

**REVIEW:**

---

**TITLE:**            **AUTHOR:**

**GENRE:**            **N° OF PAGES:**

**RATING:** ☆☆☆☆☆ **FORMAT:**

**REVIEW:**

# BOOK REVIEWS

TITLE:  AUTHOR:

GENRE:  N° OF PAGES:

RATING: ☆☆☆☆☆ FORMAT:

REVIEW:

---

TITLE:  AUTHOR:

GENRE:  N° OF PAGES:

RATING: ☆☆☆☆☆ FORMAT:

REVIEW:

# NOTES

# DECEMBER

Aslo by Warm Publishing
# No Rules
by *Anita Rigins*

**She's a runner, but the campus star quaterback runs faster than she does!**

Rocky has had a chaotic life from which she concluded three fundamental things: life is a succession of problems to be solved, men are assholes to be avoided and promises are only binding on fools who want to believe in them. So, unlike the other girls on campus, boys are not a priority for her. Worse, she sees them as an obstacle to her success!

But during a student party, she meets Jude. Freshly transferred from Harvard to play on Brown's soccer team, Jude is the new star on campus. Handsome and inaccessible, he is the type not to get attached: the perfect candidate for a one-night stand.

But the chemistry is too strong. And though Rocky is determined to run away from him, he is determined to conquer her heart.

# BOOKS TO READ

**MONTH:**
**YEAR:**

| AUTHORS | TITLES |
|---------|--------|
|         |        |
|         |        |
|         |        |
|         |        |
|         |        |
|         |        |
|         |        |
|         |        |
|         |        |
|         |        |
|         |        |
|         |        |
|         |        |
|         |        |
|         |        |
|         |        |
|         |        |
|         |        |
|         |        |

# READING CHALLENGES

# NEW RELEASES

| DATE | TITLE |
|------|-------|
|      |       |
|      |       |
|      |       |
|      |       |
|      |       |
|      |       |
|      |       |
|      |       |
|      |       |
|      |       |
|      |       |
|      |       |
|      |       |
|      |       |
|      |       |
|      |       |
|      |       |
|      |       |
|      |       |
|      |       |
|      |       |
|      |       |
|      |       |
|      |       |
|      |       |

# BOOK HAUL

# MONTHLY WRAP-UP

N° OF PAGES READ: _____

N° OF BOOKS READ: _____

N° OF E-BOOKS READ: _____

N° OF AUDIOBOOKS: _____

## BEST BOOKS:

........................................
........................................
........................................
........................................

## GENRES READ:

........................................
........................................
........................................

* ........................................
  ☆☆☆☆☆
* ........................................
  ☆☆☆☆☆
* ........................................
  ☆☆☆☆☆

* ........................................
  ☆☆☆☆☆
* ........................................
  ☆☆☆☆☆
* ........................................
  ☆☆☆☆☆
* ........................................
  ☆☆☆☆☆
* ........................................
  ☆☆☆☆☆
* ........................................
  ☆☆☆☆☆
* ........................................
  ☆☆☆☆☆
* ........................................
  ☆☆☆☆☆
* ........................................
  ☆☆☆☆☆
* ........................................
  ☆☆☆☆☆
* ........................................
  ☆☆☆☆☆

# BOOK REVIEWS

**TITLE:** **AUTHOR:**

**GENRE:** **N° OF PAGES:**

**RATING:** ☆☆☆☆☆ **FORMAT:**

**REVIEW:**

---

**TITLE:** **AUTHOR:**

**GENRE:** **N° OF PAGES:**

**RATING:** ☆☆☆☆☆ **FORMAT:**

**REVIEW:**

# BOOK REVIEWS

**TITLE:** **AUTHOR:**

**GENRE:** **N° OF PAGES:**

**RATING:** ☆☆☆☆☆ **FORMAT:**

**REVIEW:**

---

**TITLE:** **AUTHOR:**

**GENRE:** **N° OF PAGES:**

**RATING:** ☆☆☆☆☆ **FORMAT:**

**REVIEW:**

# NOTES

# FINAL WRAP-UP

## TOP 10

## STATS
BOOKS READ:

E-BOOKS READ:

AUDIOBOOKS LISTEN:

PAGES READ:

## FOR NEXT YEAR
BOOKS IN MY TBR:

E-BOOKS IN MY TBR:

AUDIOBOOKS TO LISTEN:

## HAUL
BOOKS BOUGHT:

E-BOOKS BOUGHT:

AUDIOBOOKS BOUGHT:

# YEARLY BOOK HAUL

| TITLE | FORMAT |
|---|---|
|  |  |
|  |  |
|  |  |
|  |  |
|  |  |
|  |  |
|  |  |
|  |  |
|  |  |
|  |  |
|  |  |
|  |  |
|  |  |
|  |  |
|  |  |
|  |  |
|  |  |
|  |  |
|  |  |
|  |  |
|  |  |
|  |  |

# YEARLY BOOK HAUL

| TITLE | FORMAT |
|---|---|
| | |
| | |
| | |
| | |
| | |
| | |
| | |
| | |
| | |
| | |
| | |
| | |
| | |
| | |
| | |
| | |
| | |
| | |
| | |
| | |
| | |
| | |

## NOTES

# NOTES

# NOTES

# NOTES

# NOTES

# NOTES

# NOTES

# NOTES

# NOTES

www.ingramcontent.com/pod-product-compliance
Lightning Source LLC
Chambersburg PA
CBHW061119070526
44583CB00028B/3342